Colmar, the most beautiful city in the world ?

With just a hint of provocation in your voice, you say to me, using a fairly repugnant spot of ink to cast a delicious shadow, you say to me that Colmar is the most beautiful city in Alsace. Well, my friend, you've got it wrong: Colmar is quite simply the most beautiful city in the world...

You shrug your shoulders with annoyance. You snap off the tip of your pencil; you send me all kinds of little signs to show me that while enthusiasm may be praiseworthy, a sense of perspective still needs to be kept. What do you want me to say? The truth, first of all, even when it is absurd, even when it is unjust. I am forced to repeat that you are, this morning, the best of all friends and that Colmar, now, is the most beautiful city in the world...

Georges Duhamel, 1931.

Tourist Attractions

The House of the Heads

Built in 1609 for a local merchant, Anton Burger, the Maison des Têtes is a fine example of the German renaissance and owes its name to the grotesque masks or heads that decorate the rich façade. A superb oriel window rises over 3 floors of the house and the gable is topped with a statue of a cooper, sculpted by Bartholdi (1902).

The village of Hansi and his museum

28 rue des Têtes is located the museum dedicated to the artiste Jean-Jaques Waltz, called "Hansi". It brings to life the fascinating world of the painter who was devoted to the Alsatian region. On 700 m², discover the village of Hansi as seen in his lovely paintings. Don't miss the museum coffee shop and Uncle Hansi's market place, with a large offer of regional products.

This museum offers a journey through nearly 7,000 years of history, from Prehistory to the art of the 20th century. In the mediaeval cloister, we find the art of the Middel Ages, the Renaissance and the unmissable masterpiece, the Issenheim Altarpiece by Matthias Grünewald. The former municipal baths provide a space conducive to temporary exhibits and the new contemporary wing forms the showcase for major artists of the 20th century.

Town library

After the Second World War, the library of Colmar was moved into the old Dominican monastery, in which can be seen a very fine mediaeval cloister. The library is remarkably rich, housing over 1,200 manuscripts, the oldest of which dates back to the 8th century, as well as some 3,000 Rhenish, French and Italian incunabula.

Dominican church

The great nave, with its wooden ceiling, supported by slender columns without capitals, is reminiscent of the hall churches of the time and is one of the finest examples of the architecture of the Holy Roman Empire's mendicant orders. Completed in 1346, the church belonged to the Dominicans of Colmar, who achieved a certain fame in the 14th century when they initiated the reform of the Dominican order, intended to bring members of the order back to stricter observance of the original rule, and which was applied over the whole of the Empire.

Voltaire's residence

Voltaire stayed in this house for 13 months, from 1753-1754. He stopped off in Colmar to finish his Annales de l'Empire, the writing of which had been interrupted by his quarrel with Frederick II and his subsequent expulsion from the court. The exceptionally rich libraries of the lawyers and councillors of the Sovereign Court meant he was able to complete his book in Colmar.

Bartholdi Museum

The house where the famous sculptor Frédéric Auguste Bartholdi was born in 1834. The house was built in the 15th century and converted in the 18th century. It now houses the largest display devoted to the life and works of the creator of the statue of Liberty.

In the courtyard, visitors can see Bartholdi's Grands soutiens du monde, cast in bronze in 1902.

Pfister house

One of the symbols of old Colmar, the maison Pfister bears the name of a 19th century owner of the house. Built in 1537 by Ludwig Scherer, a hatmaker, the house is made of stone and wood and its mediaeval design includes a long wooden gallery and an angular oriel window rising over 2 floors. The house is decorated in the Renaissance style, while the paintings on the façade represent the Germanic emperors of the 16th century, the Evangelists, the Fathers of the Church and allegorical figures along with biblical figures and scenes.

Adolph house

This house is considered to be one of the oldest in Colmar. It is named after the owner who uncovered the Gothic windows in the second half of the 19th cetury.

The 2nd floor windows are reminiscent of those of St. Martin's collegiate church, which date back to the same period.

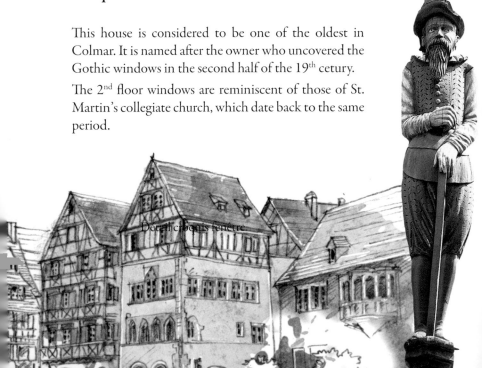

Détail croquis fenêtre

The former Guard House

The site was originally occupied by the St. James' Chapel, part of the neighbouring St. Martin's cemetery. It was converted into a guard house in 1575. The portal and the loggia are splendid examples of upper Rhine Renaissance architecture.

Saint Martin Collegiate church

St. Martin's Collegiate church was built between 1235 and 1365 and is a major example of Gothic architecture in Alsace. The south tower was burnt down in a fire in 1572 that also destroyed its framework and ridge. It was replaced 3 years later by the bulb-shaped dome that gives the building its characteristic appearance. The church has been restored several times, the latest restoration works ended in 1982. The foundations of a church dating back to the end of the first millennium were found, along with traces of building work from the 11th and 12th centuries during the restoration. St. Martin's was also the seat of a constitutional bishopric between 1791 and 1802.

Town Hall

Built ten years before the Revolution, the Town Hall was originally the town residence for the Cistercian abbey of Pairis, situated some 20 kilometers from Colmar in the Val d'Orbey. It housed the departmental administrative offices as from 1790 and then the Préfecture of the Haut-Rhin (Upper Rhine) between 1800 and 1866, before becoming the Town Hall of Colmar.

Seat of the Ploughmen's guild

This handsome Renaissance building, with its majestic portal, was used as a meeting hall by the powerful farmers' guild, before being taken over by the Jewish community for religious services before the construction of the synagogue. In the centre of the frieze, you can make out the inscription EH VERACHT ALS GEMACHT 1626, which means "faster undone than done".

13 Synagogue

The synagogue was built from 1839 to 1842, in a pseudo-antique style and is the seat of the Israelite Consistory and the Grand Rabbinate of the Haut-Rhin. The Jewish community first moved to Colmar in the 13th century. Expelled from the city in the 16th century, they returned after the Revolution.

14 Former Hospital

When the Franciscans moved out of Colmar in the 16th century, their monastery was converted into a hospital. The French monarchy built a new hospital between 1736 and 1744, using stones from the city fortifications, which had been demolished in 1673. The hospital would remain in use until 1937, when it was replaced by the Pasteur hospital, in the west of the city.

Saint Matthew's Church

This Franciscan church was built in the late 12th century and underwent substantial restoration a few years ago to bring it back to its former glory. Along with the Dominican church, it is one of the major examples of churches of the mendicant orders in Alsace.

St. Matthew's became a Protestant church after the Reformation was introduced in Colmar in 1575 and its superb acoustics mean it is often now used as a concert hall, notably for the Colmar International Music Festival.

Former protestant presbytery

This Renaissance building was constructed in 1606, and features a row of arcades
housing boutiques at street level and
two angular oriel windows rising over
the three floors of the façade looking
out onto the Grand'Rue. It was built
for Protestant ministers from the nearby
church.

Tanners' District

The Tanners' District underwent detailed restoration between 1968 and 1974. The district was listed as a historical monument in 1966 under the famous Malraux law and continues to attract hundreds of thousands of visitors from all over the world. The district is a sort of village of its own within the city, with high, half-timbered houses mostly dating back to the 17th and 18th centuries. The houses were used by tanners for drying out their skins on the open upper floors.

18 Schwendi fountain ☾

The Schwendi fountain, designed by Bartholdi, was built in 1898, and represents Lazare de Schwendi, a warlord who fought for the Empire and
who was also the seigneur of nearby Hohlandsbourg. Schwendi fought
against the Turks in Hungary. He is to be seen grasping a Tokay vine stock
that he is supposed to have brought back from his campaigns. In actual fact,
the Alsatian "Tokay" is none other than the Pinot Gris grape, that has been
used in winemaking in the region since the Middle Ages.

"Koïfhus" former Customs House

The Koïfhus was the old commercial and economic focal point of Colmar and was completed in 1480. It is the oldest local public building in the city. The old Renaissance balustrade, removed some 20 years ago, has now been restored, thus giving the Koïfhus back its original appearance. The ground floor was used as a warehouse and for levying tax on imported and exported merchandise. The first floor was a meeting room for representatives of the Décapole, the federation of the ten Imperial towns of Alsace, that was created in 1354.

Tourist Attractions

Law court

The building was designed by Chassain and Rungs in a classical style, to house the Sovereign Council of Alsace, the High Court of Justice and the regional parliament, which had been set up in Colmar in 1698. Completed in 1771, the building now houses the regional law court, after being the seat of the Colmar Court of Appeal until the beginning of the 20th century. Colmar is still the judicial capital of the region and is the seat of the Court of Appeal for both Rhine departments.

Monument dedicated to Pfeffel

Théophile Conrad Pfeffel (1736-1749), was a poet and teacher, who wrote well-known fables and founded the famous "Military Academy". His statue was the work of Charles Geiss and was erected in 1927. It is actually a copy of the original, made by André Friedrich in 1859 for the Unterlinden Museum.

The covered market

The covered market was built by Parisian architect Louis-Michel Boltz, between 1863 and 1865. It is made of bricks and stone and has metal frames held up by cast-iron columns. The building is still used as a market and every Thursday the surrounding area, through the Tanners' district behind the Koïfhus, fills with a colourful array of stalls. The recess in the south-western angle houses Bartholdi's statue of a winemaker (1869).

The Fishmongers' district

The fishmongers' and fishermen's guild was once a powerful body in Colmar. Up to the beginning of the 20th century, they would sell their fish, caught locally, on the quay front. The district was thoroughly restored between 1978 and 1981 and provides the link between the Tanners' district and the picturesque "Little Venice".

Natural History Museum

The natural history museum houses a rich collection of zoological, mineral and ethnographical specimens. The building had previously housed the Turenne school and was converted to a museum in 1985. It is run by the Société d'histoire naturelle, which, along with the Société Schongauer, which runs the Unterlinden museum, is one of the oldest of Colmar's associations.

Little Venice

Little Venice, which is as popular as ever with tourists, owes its name to the way the houses are lined up on either side of the Lauch. It is in the heart of the Krutenau market-garden district, which extends along the rue Turenne, the road taken by Marshal Turenne when he marched triumphantly into the city in 1674.

26

Former St. John "Commanderie"

There remains little of the original Commandery of the Knights Hospitallers of St. John of Jerusalem; which was built here in the 13th century. A few vestiges can still be seen in the façades overlooking the street and the courtyard. The building underwent substantial change in the 19th century and is now used as a private school.

The House of the St. John's Knight

This house, inaccurately described as once belonging to the Knights of St. John, was built upon the model of a Venetian mansion, with two wings at right angles to the street, enclosing a courtyard overlooked by two floors of galleries and balustrades. Built in 1608 and pulled down in the 19th century, the house has been rebuilt to the original specifications.

The statue of Provost Marshal Jean Roesselmann was sculpted by Bartholdi in 1888. Roesselman died when successfully defending Colmar and the city's liberties against the troops and ambitions of the Bishop of Strasbourg, in 1262. Our hero bears the features of Hercule de Peyerimhoff, a former Mayor of Colmar who was unceremoniously booted out of office in 1877 for refusing to submit to the German authorities.

Bartholdi College

The buildings were once the Jesuit college and were completed in 1720. The Jesuits were expelled in 1765 and the buildings became the collège royal, the central school of the Haut Rhin in 1796 and subsequently the lycée impérial in 1856. The north wing was built by architect Pierre Michel d'Ixnard, who designed therein the highly original salle des actes (theatre) and the school's library.

30 St. Peter's Chapel

The priory of St. Peter originally belonged to the Benedictine abbey of Payerne in Switzerland. It was built on the Oberhof, one of the primitive cores of Colmar, in the 10th century. A twin-towered Romanesque church, which can be seen in the earliest pictures of the city, was built on the site in the 12th century, before being replaced by the Jesuit chapel, built by Strasbourg architect Jean-Paul Sarger between 1742 and 1750.

Monument dedicated to Hirn

Gustave Adolphe Hirn, a physician, astronomer, mathematician and philosopher (1815-1890), is the greatest scientist in Colmar's long history. His research into thermodynamics and oil made him a pioneer of modern industry. His statue is by Bartholdi and was inaugurated just four years after Hirn's death, in 1894.

Water tower

Colmar's water tower is the oldest existing water tower in Alsace. Built in the neo-Gothic German style, it has been a feature of the Colmar landscape since 1886. It is 53 metres high and can contain up to 1200 m³ of water. It has not been used since 1984.

"St. Martin's Circle"

The curious neo-Gothic building of the cercle Saint Martin was completed in 1895, to be used for sports and cultural activities in St. Martin's parish. The church had come up with a vast programme aimed at young people and the majority of the great cultural events in the inter-war period were held in the building.

Monument dedicadet to Bartholdi

Auguste Bartholdi (1834-1904), created the design for the Statue of Liberty and the Lion of Belfort. With Schongauer, he was the most prolific of Colmar's artists and richly deserves his own monument. The statue was unveiled in 1907 in front of an impressive array of notables and was designed by Hubert Louis-Noël and Antoine Rubin.

Court of Appeal

The Court of Appeal is another typical example of German architecture of the early 20th century. The Courthouse was finished in 1906 and its impressive volume now houses the highest court in Alsace, the descendant of the old Sovereign Council of Alsace, which had made Colmar the judicial capital of the region, in 1698.

Prefecture

The Colmar préfecture was originally to be found in what is now the Town Hall, in the rue des clefs. In 1866 it moved into the present building, designed in the Louis XIII style of architecture, and facing the Champ de Mars park, which is laid out in a cross-shape like that of the Légion d'honneur.

A. J. BRUAT
AMIRAL DE FRANCE

1796 · 1855

Bruat Fountain

The Bartholdi-designed Bruat fountain was inaugurated in 1864, and is surmounted by a statue of Admiral Armand-Joseph Bruat (1796-1855). The fountain represents the allegories of the four continents and was destroyed by the Nazis in 1940, to be rebuilt in 1958. The original sandstone heads are to be found in the Bartholdi museum. Alfred Schweitzer wrote that the head of the African was what inspired him to be a doctor in the African bush.

Monument to General Rapp

This statue of General Rapp (1771-1821) was Bartholdi's first public monument and was exhibited initially on the Champs-Elysées in Paris. It was then shown at the Universal Exhibition of Paris in 1855 before being moved to Colmar in 1856. Today it stands proudly over the eponymous square, which has been renovated and is now a pedestrian-only zone.

AU GENERAL RAPP

The "Catherinettes"

Once the convent of the Dominican nuns of St. Catherine, this building has seen considerable changes over the centuries and is now used both for local events and as a school, as well as being the administrative building of the local tourist office. The apse of the choir was removed in the 19th century to allow for work on the rue Kléber. The elegantly restored pinnacle now bears witness to the building's original purpose.

Theatre

The municipal theatre neighbouring the former unterlinden convent was completed in 1849, and was designed in the Italian style by Parisian architect Louis Michel Boltz. The interior, with its remarkable ceiling paintwork, is the work of another Parisian, Boulangé. Painstaking restoration work was finished in 2000 and the theatre can now be seen as it was when first built.

Museum of toys and little trains

The last of Colmar's museums, but
certainly not the least. With over 70,000
visitors per year, it's one of Alsace's top-
ranked museums. Toys hold pride of
place, with model trains in the forefront.
Don't miss the temporary exhibitions,
they're often absolute gems.

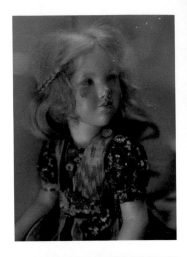

"Espace Malraux"

A centre for Contemporary Art, housed in an old sauerkraut factory, the
espace MALRAUX boasts a top-ranking programme of exhibitions for the
general public. It has played an important role in giving Colmar its modern
identity.

To develop and to bring the heritage to life

Indeed Colmar possesses a wealth of architectural treasures dating from various periods. None should be shown off to the detriment of another, nor should the warm romantic after-dark atmosphere of this most enchanting district be spoilt.

Today, 1,100 computer-controlled points of light are scattered throughout the town providing illuminations that highlight its streets, architectural details on facades and small bridges. During the year the decor varies by magical changes in colours.

The town is illuminated from nightfall on Fridays and Saturdays throughout the whole year, and every evening during major events marking the life in Colmar: the International Festival, Regional Alsace Wine Fair and Christmas in Colmar.

Colmar International Festival

Christmas magic in Colmar

Christmas sees a vast celebration of the festive season in Alsace, with Colmar in the forefront. The architectural and historical heritage of the city offers an exceptional backdrop to the Christmas lighting and decoration that flourishes all though its pedestrian areas. Christmas markets fill the air with the heady aromas of mulled wine and gingerbread, while concerts and other Yuletide entertainments abound. Colmar is the ideal starting point for a trip round the surrounding mediaeval villages, many of which, dressed up in their Christmas costumes, offer the visitor an unusual and highly original picture of a region in full festive flow.

ex eo qd̄ narro. n̄ aliud qua ueritatē inq̄rere. n̄
ud qua diuina ueritatē diligere. n̄ aliū qua dn̄
q̄di st̄ uendicare: Solis aduersariis di resistens. so
p̄fanatorib' ꞇ p̄fanationib' cunctis obuius existens.
lis contradicentib' ueritati amore ueritatis adu
sans. hec ago ut cū uita ista q̄ temptatio super te
est fatigauerit egrū ueritas
que ds̄ e regat saluan
ꞇ in scta sctēq̄ possi
a oͦ. In cap libell
titulat̄ in laud
uirginis editur

Ildefonsus

defonso epͦo

OͦIͦRͦAͦ me
dnatrix me
dn̄ns in ma
dn̄i mei ancil
filii tui genit
factoris mundi t
go. te queso. te oro.
bei spiritū dn̄i tui
bei spͫ filii tui. habe
redēptoris mundi ut de
uera ꞇ digna sapia de te uera ꞇ digna loq̄r. de
uera & digna q̄cūq̄ st̄ diligā. Tu electa ado. assū
ado. ad uocata adeo. p̄uia adherens dͦo ciunct
dͦo uisitata ab angͦo. salutata ab angͦo. benedicta
ab angͦo. beatificata ab angͦo. turbata

The milestones of a richly contrasting history

• **823** : First mention of Colmar.

The fisc of Columbarium

The first traces of Colmar date back to 823, when Louis the Pious, son of Charlemagne, drew up an act of donation in Frankfurt on 12 June. The Carolingian monarch gave part of the forest located within the Columbarium, a vast domain that he owned in the region, to the abbey of Munster.

The name Colmar is of Roman origin. It actually means dovecote, the place where doves are bred and raised. There are a lot of towns and villages in France with the same etymology, such as Colombes and Coulommiers. Roman villas are almost certainly to be found around the Colmar area. The mosaic from the Gallo-Roman villa in Bergheim , which was discovered in the 19th century, actually led to the creation of the Unterlinden Museum.

The nearest town in the Roman era was Argentovaria, a fortified camp built by the Emperor Valentinian in the 4th century a.d. in an unsuccessful attempt to stop German raids. In the Frankish period, the economic centre shifted west-wards and there was frequent flooding as the unpredictable river Ill spilt over into the surrounding countryside. The Barbarians knew the fortified camp as Horbourg, the fortress of mud, and preferred to settle along the drier, fertile lands running along the Ill.

When the Franks conquered Gaul in the 5th and 6th centuries, they kept aside great swathes of land, including the area around Colmar, to provide food. Nobody can actually say, however, if Colmar was founded in the Merovingian or Carolingian period.

What was it like in its earliest days? According to French historian Charles Wilsdorf, it would have been made up of "a set of large wooden and cobwork buildings, with a more sophisticated construction in the centre, built with a vast storeroom, that would shelter the sovereign and his court when they stayed there. The settlement would also include various outhouses, such as barns, stables, a press, the kitchen, a bakery, a farmyard, a dovecote and the gynaeceum for the womenfolk." The Emperors of the time were constantly on the move, riding from one part of their territory to another, feeding off the produce of each domain. The Empire was a vast area and the Emperor would often go far afield, depending on the mood of the time or the political situation. There was a whole network of tracks and settlements for him to travel through, and Colmar was part of the great itinerary.

• **833 :** Unhappy with the arrangements made for the succession, Louis, Lothar and Pepin, depose their father, Louis the Pious, in the Lügenfel, the so-called field of lies, situated near Colmar. They receive the backing of Pope Gregory, who visited the domain of Colmar in July 833.

• **883 :** Charles 3rd, known as Charles the Fat, holds an assembly of all the Franks in January of 883 and then again in February 884. All the important figures in the Empire were invited, representing the countries between the Meuse and the Elbe as well as those from over the Alps and from the north of Italy.

Crucifixion, missel de l'abbaye de Murbach, vers 1200.
Bibliothèque Municipale de Colmar.

• **Ca. 965 :** The Oberhof ("upper court"), part of the old royal Carolingian domain, comes under the Clunisian monastery of Payerne (situated in the Swiss canton of Vaud), while a second part, the Niederhof (lower court), becomes the property of Bishop Conrad of Constance, who gave it to the cathedral chapter of his Episcopal town.

• **Ca. 1000 :** Archaeological digs carried out in 1972 in St. Mark's church revealed that Colmar had its own "millennium church", made up of a square apse, a transept 19 metres long and 8 metres wide, along with a nave 15 metres long, consisting of a central body flanked by two aisles.

- **1002** : Brunon of Eguisheim, the future Pope Leo IX, is born in Eguisheim, a few miles outside Colmar. Leo IX was the only Alsatian Pope and was canonised shortly after his death.

- **1106** : Colmar is destroyed by a fire.

- **1153** : On 30 January, Frederick Barbarossa stops off at Colmar for the first time. He would return in 1156, 1179 and 1186.

- **1212** : King Philip of Swabia passes through Colmar.

- **1226** : Documents cite Colmar as a city for the first time, a few years after being made an imperial town by Frederick II of Hohenstaufen.

- **1234** : The building of St. Martin's collegiate church starts, to be finished in 1365.

- **1235** : Emperor Frederick II visits the city and, according to the chronicler of the Colmar Dominicans, makes a big impression with the camels included in his imperial baggage.

- **1262** : Provost Jean Roesselmann, who had freed the inhabitants of Colmar from the yoke of the Bishop of Strasbourg the previous year, fights off a fresh attack by the latter, but at the cost of his own life.

- **1278** : King Rudolph of Hapsburg gives Colmar its civil rights.

Saint Francis and Saint Dominic, breviary for the laity, 15ᵗʰ century
Library of the Protestant Consistory of Colmar.

The Colmar civil rights charter

A drier document than this charter, dated 29 December 1278, would be hard to find. It is signed by Rudolph of Hapsburg, who was at the time in Vienna. The initial impression is of a list of 44 prescriptions, without any logical order and drawn from penal law, private law and procedures. The document is, however, of prime importance for the history of the city. The Freiheitsbrief, laid down the laws to consolidate the city's position and give some structure to the relations between the inhabitants. It was the first act to put the law down in writing and goes into detail on points which previously relied on prior privilege, but which had never been actually set out.

The document was written in German and aimed to strengthen the city's autonomy. It made the burghers masters of their own destiny, with the right to draw up legislation in the interests of the city. The Schultheiss held executive power, but its incumbent had to be a burgher from Colmar and reside in the city of Colmar. This condition effectively removed any "foreign" takeover of the city, at least as far as the law was concerned.

The charter also gave the burghers of Colmar the right to own fiefs, which had previously been the exclusive privilege of the nobility, thereby removing a barrier between nobles and commoners. Any man, even a serf, could become a burgher. The lord had a year to lay claim on the serf and once the year was up, the serf became a free man, according to the adage Stadtluft macht frei. Noble burghers, serving the king, did not have to pay tax. Others, the Uzburger, or outside burghers, did not have to reside permanently in the city. The Council and the Schultheiss appointed two citizens of proven integrity, chosen from the bourgeoisie, to check weights and measures. This decision had a significant impact on the food (corn, flour, wine) and trade (gold, silver) sectors.

The penal provisions provide first-hand evidence of the judicial and moral climate reigning in the city at the time, with their archaic and sometimes genuinely violent undertones. Any murder within Colmar was to be punished by decapitation and the demolition of the guilty party's house. Judicial duelling was common, but restricted to burghers. No one from outside the civic boundaries could challenge a burgher to a duel. Lex talionis, or an eye for an eye, was legally recognised. These are just a few examples from the document, which was considered so important that it was used as the basis for charters that the Hapsburg princes would grant to other towns and cities, such as Delle, Ensisheim, Kaysersberg, Mulhouse, Munster and Turckheim and, outside Alsace, Aarau, Neuchatel, Petit-Bâle, Porrentruy and Fribourg in Brisgau.

The two-headed eagle of the Hapsburgs at the Koïfhus (Old Customs House), 15th c.

Dominican convent of Unterlinden by Henri Lebert in 1838.
Unterlinden Museum.

- **1293** : Colmar rises up unsuccessfully against Adolf of Nassau.

- **1295** : The city's first town hall.

- **1337** : First mention of Ladhof, the port of Colmar.

Ladhof, the port of Colmar, stands some two kilometers to the north of the city, at the confluence of the Thur and the Lauch, at the spot where the river Ill becomes navigable. First mentions of Ladhof appeared in 1337, and it continued to be used as a port until the 18th century. Goods were loaded onto boats for Strasbourg and then taken on along the Rhine right up to Amsterdam. Colmar merchants would sail up the Rhine once a year to the great fairs in Frankfurt. Ladhof, literally "the place where merchandise is loaded", was the port for their wine, vinegar and schnapps and was also used for unloading iron utensils and the salted and smoked fish which was greatly prized in Colmar.

- **Ca. 1340** : Catherine of Gueberschwihr describes the life of the nuns of the Dominican convent of Unterlinden.

- **1354** : Foundation of the Décapole, a Federation of the ten Alsatian cities, with Colmar at its head.

The Décapole

Colmar was one of the ten cities comprising the famous league of the Décapole, and which still proudly claim their membership even today. Popular imagination would have the Décapole representing a time when cities preferred to act together rather than tear each other apart. The Décapole was the first association of communes of the region and would survive right up till the French Revolution. It has now passed into local legend and mythology. The real story, however, is a little different.

Towns and cities in the 14th century led a precarious existence and were under continual pressure from local barons. They had been granted certain privileges by the Emperor, but remained in a parlous state of fragility. They realised that to avoid baronial domination and retain their relative freedom under imperial protection, they had to group together to offer mutual help. 7 Alsatian towns had already formed a league in 1342, with the approval of Emperor Charles IV, who was also a prime mover in the foundation of the confederation of the ten imperial cities of Alsace on 28 August 1354.

Wissembourg, Haguenau, Rosheim, Obernai, Sélestat Kaysersberg, Colmar, Munster, Turckheim and Mulhouse joined together to form a united front to defend their privileges and status of Imperial cities. The cities agreed on a mutual protection pact if any of them should come under attack from outside or experience internal difficulties.

They were realistic enough to realise that a conflict could pit some of them against each other and so they undertook to resolve all such disputes amicably. They also made sure that membership of the confederation did not stand in the way of their freedom to act and to exist.

Annunciation, Collection of sermons..., 15th c. Colmar municipal library.

There was no hierarchy or subordination in the Décapole, with all the cities enjoying equal ranking. Haguenau, where the *Landvogt* (Imperial Governer) had resided and ruled over the imperial domain in Alsace since the 13th century, was recognised as the administrative centre. Colmar, by far the biggest of the cities, and Haguenau sent deputies to represent the Décapole at the imperial diets and assemblies of imperial cities. The Emperor's protection also gave the cities a certain degree of military backing and when the need arose, troops were drafted from the cities and placed under the authority of the *Landvogt*. On the judicial side, the imperial glove could also be seen at work in resolving disputes. A disagreement between an imperial town or city and an "immediate" domain or between a municipal government and the burghers of the city would be arbitrated by the Haguenau authorities. Colmar, by joining the Décapole, demonstrated its freedom and its solidarity with the other cities. By then, it was the second largest imperial city in Alsace, behind Strasbourg, which enjoyed the status of a free city.

- **1360** : Colmar adopts a stable constitution, with the city being governed by its burghers and members of the guilds.

- **1376** : The city wins the right to mint its own coinage.

- **1389** : Colmar is chosen by Robert de Capoue, Grand Master of the Dominicans, as the base for the Dominican reform aimed at bringing the order back to a stricter observance of the rules and spirit of the original constitutions in the Domincan province of Teutonia.

- **1403** : The city joins the Rappen-münzbund monetary alliance.

- **1418** : The bubonic plague strikes Colmar.

- **1473** : Martin Schongauer paints the Virgin of the Rose Bower for St. Martin's collegiate church.

- **1480** : The Koïfhus or Customs House is completed. The building has a triple use, as a store for Colmar merchants and tradesmen, as a customs office for the city to levy its duties and taxes and also as an assembly room for the Décapole representatives.

Colmar Trutzthaler, 1666.

Martin Schongauer's Virgin of the Rose Bower, 1473.
Colmar Dominican church.

- **1512 :** The Jewish community is brutally thrown out of Colmar and not allowed to return until the Revolution. Jews had been living in Colmar since the 13th century and were active in both the economic and cultural life of the city. A number of them were massacred during the plague of 1349.

- **1521 :** The city's statutes are changed and the number of guilds cut from twenty to ten.

- **1522-1525 :** Colmar finds itself in the middle of an intellectual, social and religious upheaval. It becomes a centre of Lutheran propaganda, with works pouring off the presses of the Farckall print shop. The city just managed to avoid the violent struggles of the Peasant war.

- **1528 :** Paracelsis, the alchemist physician, finds refuge in Colmar before continuing on his wanderings.

- **1536 :** The city acquires the nearby seigniory of Sainte-Croix-en-plaine.

- **1538 :** After a number of scandals, the Magistrat or government of Colmar publishes a Klosterordnung that lays down the rules for the clerics living in the monasteries.

The Koïfhus in 1840, drawing by J. Rothmuller, lithograph by E. Simon fils, Strasbourg.

• **1548** : The German writer Georges Wickram, considered to be the originator of the popular novel in German, sets up a reputed singing school (Meistersingerschule) in Colmar.

Colmar is a pleasant city...

It is situated on a fertile plain, far from the mountains, an hour along the track, with large quantities of wine and grain on either side, and the land is good for wheat, onions and other fruit of the garden. This city is in the centre of Alsace and is a single league away from Keisersperg, Ammersweiler, Rechenwyer and Rappoltzweyer, towns that make most excellent wine, the finest of all Alsace.

Sébastien Münster, Cosmographie, 1552

Colmar standard-bearer,
Wappenbuch of J. Koebel,
Frankfurt, 1545.

• **1575** : Colmar comes under the Lutheran reform. The public authorities offer the Protestant community use of the Franciscan church.

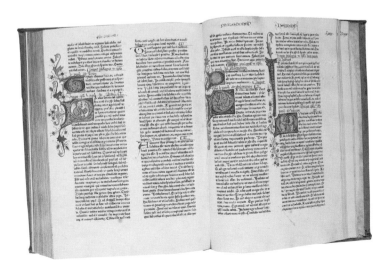

Mentelin's Latin bible, 1459-1460. First major book printed in Alsace.
Colmar Municipal Library .

The introduction of the Reformation

The first evangelical service held in Colmar took place on 15 May 1575, at 8 o'clock in the morning, in the Franciscan church, which had lain empty for the previous thirty years. The city's governing class were present in great number. As no minister had yet been appointed to the Protestant community, the minister of Jebsheim, Jean Cellarius, officiated. The decision to allow the service to go ahead had only been taken the day before, when the City council met under the chairmanship of Obristmeister Michel Buob to give its unanimous vote of approval.

It had been a long wait for the Colmar Protestants, who had thought the Reformation would be introduced in 1525, some 50 years before. The public authorities had shown a singular mastery of procrastination, surrounding themselves with a panoply of judicial precautions before finally giving the go-ahead at the last moment. Colmar was known as a eine spät Reformationsstadt, a late reformation city. The city's rulers had long prevaricated, leaving Colmar half a century behind Strasbourg and Basel in joining the Reformation. It would take the city another fifty years to decide between Luther and Calvin.

In 1525, the peasants' war had come to its tragic end and this cooled Colmar's ardour for introducing the Reformation. The public authorities were very half-hearted in their support, even though part of the population showed sympathy for the new ideas. Farckall's Lutheran publications, the problem with Hans the preacher and the innkeeper Bader's incitements to sedition showed that for all the hesitation, Colmar still had a toe placed firmly in the waters of the Reformation.

It was not until the Peace of Augsburg in 1555, however, that the Reformation started to gain wider acceptance in Colmar although it had been widely introduced in the surrounding areas. Through a decree issued in 1538, the Public authorities had managed to gain control of administering the possessions and regulating the practices of the clergy. The Reformation had also lost ground through the excesses of the Anabaptists and the counter-reformation work of Catholics like Jean Fabbri, the Dominican preacher of St. Martin and the Augustinian prior Jean Hoffmeister.

The city's situation finally began to change with the Peace of Augsburg. This peace officially recognised the coexistence of Catholicism and Lutheranism throughout the Empire, the introduction of the Reformation in Haguenau in 1565 and the new governing body in Colmar in 1564, which brought in new faces and new ideas. There was now no danger, either politically or domestically, in introducing the Reformation.

• **1580** : New fortifications, designed by Strasbourg architect Specklin, are built.

Colmar - imperial city

The free imperial city of Colmar. The illustrious magistrate offered us lunch and served us wine with toasts. Two ministers of the church sat at the meal, in the name of the City.

The city is well fortified; it is surrounded by a double moat and a double rampart and possesses an elegant arsenal.

Wolfgang Meyer, minister in Basel and Mulhouse, 1618

• **1627** : The Thirty Years War is in full sway and Protestantism is banned in Colmar. It will be re-introduced in 1632, under the Swedish occupation.

• **1635** : The Treaty of Rueil, signed on 1 August 1635, places Colmar under the protection of the King of France. The city keeps its status of Imperial city, its franchises, privileges, rights and customs and, even better, when the war is over, it should be restored to its previous position, as set out in the elegant wording of the Treaty, "the said city shall be restored to the condition which it enjoyed before the beginning of the troubles of Germany and Bohemia in 1618".

• **1648** : The Treaty of Munster in Westphalia gives part of Alsace over to France. Colmar, like all the other cities of the Décapole, remains an Imperial city. The French troops move out of Colmar.

Title page of the Apologia of the Imperical City of Colmar, published by D. Imlin and J.B Schneider, Colmar 1645.

The Treaties of Westphalia

These treaties were of immense importance for the history of Alsace and of Colmar. They put an end to a conflict that had been tearing Europe apart since 1618, recognised the victory of Sweden and France and hastened the end of the Holy Roman Empire.

There were in fact two treaties of Westphalia. The first one, drawn up between Sweden and the Empire in Osnabrück, laid down religious tolerance across the Empire. Goods and rights were to be restored to those who held them on 1st January 1624, the "standard year". Members of the Reformed church (Calvinist) were to enjoy the same rights as those granted to the Lutherans in the Peace of 1555.

The second treaty, drawn up in Munster, had a more political slant. It gave France, a latecomer to the war, the chance to push up some important pawns on the diplomatic chessboard. The preliminary peace agreement of 13 September 1648 gave France the Hapsburgs' possessions in Alsace, while the imperial cities would remain within the immediacy of the Empire.

When the treaties were signed, on 24 October 1648, nothing much had changed, despite intensive diplomacy and the efforts of people such as Balthasar Schneider of Colmar. The King of France had won ownership of the Hapsburg lands in Alsace, which made up about four fifths of Upper Alsace. The House of Austria had ceded to France the Sundgau and Brisach, the Austrian seigniories with Ensisheim and the landgraviat (principality) of Upper Alsace. The landgraviat of Lower Alsace also came under the French crown, along with the great imperial bailiwick which had been in Hapsburg hands since 1558 and it was to this great bailiwick that belonged the forty villages and ten imperial towns and cities of the Décapole.

View of Colmar by Mérian in 1644. Haut-Rhin departmental archives.

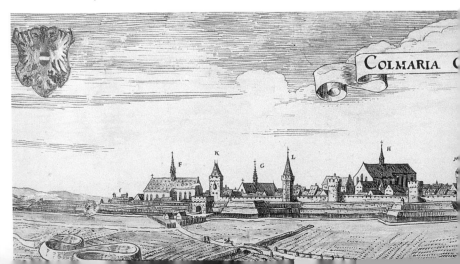

The threat was therefore very real and it appeared that the Décapole towns could be split from the Empire. The Treaty of Munster, however, showed itself to be a true child of diplomatic ambiguity, giving the barons, cities and towns of Alsace the paradoxical and parallel "immediacy of the Empire", just like under the Hapsburgs. The equivocal sentence that followed revealed the limits of the concession: "without the sovereign rights of the King being in any way reduced".

The Treaty of Munster was one step in the gradual integration of Alsace within France. Its contradictions left it wide open to varying interpretations, which allowed Colmar and the other members of the Décapole the frail, lingering hope that they could remain within the Empire. The Alsace question had begun...

Portrait of Colmar-born diplomat Balthasar, 1650.

This city is truly beautiful
and decorated with handsome buildings and edifices, situated within a beautiful and fertile plain. It is well fortified and possesses a handsome rampart. The Town Hall, the Kauffhaus and many public buildings are well constructed. There are for now no more than 13 to 14,000 burghers, most of them grown wealthy from the trade they make and from the fairs and markets held in the city. It is so well positioned that more than 40 towns and 240 villages come to the market to return home to their beds the same day.

Domilliers, subdelegate of the Intendant, ca.1660.

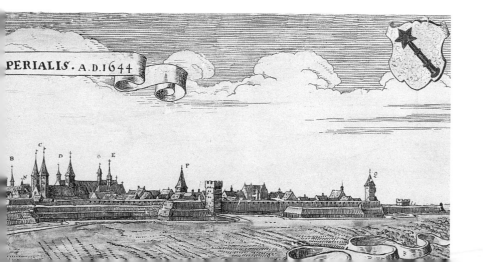

- **1673 :** The Dutch War sees the city occupied by troops of the King of France. The fortifications are destroyed and Colmar becomes an open city.

"On Wednesday 30 August, the Royal retinue, with over 200 coaches, rode in. It was 11 in the morning. Louis XIV rode around the place. In Andolsheim, where the court dined, Mlle de Montpensier, the Duchess of Orleans, noted down the words of the King: 'Messieurs les Colmariens are no longer as glorious as they once were".

The demolition work continued unabated, with over 4,000 men knocking the fortifications down. Sappers blew up the towers and walls. On Saturday 2 September, the King stopped off at Colmar, on his way back from Brisach, to see how the demolition was going. When cheered by the soldiers, he cried out "Courage, courage, mes enfants !"

- **1679 :** Under the Treaty of Nijmegen, Colmar becomes a "Royal city of France".

Colmar in 1737, engraving published by A. Muller, Haut-Rhin departmental archives.

The Royal city

"The strongest will win". So declared Dr. Volmar who was working for Austria when the Treaty of Munster was being negotiated. The ambiguities in the treaty of Westphalia meant that only force could resolve the situation. The Décapole had for a long time tried to get by on bluff alone, with Colmar showing itself to be especially intransigent. In 1651 and 1659, the city tried to get its imperial privileges restored. It had continued to contribute to the Holy Roman Empire's war against Turkey, through the famous Turkenhilfe. In 1666, the city minted a thaler showing a view of the city, its arms and the imperial eagle, a visible sign that it still belonged to the Empire. The city refused to recognize the competence of the sovereign Council, which set up in Ensisheim in 1658. Colmar resisted, sure that it would be able to argue its way out.

The political situation grew darker in 1670, with the Dutch War. The Holy Roman Empire, Spain, Brandenburg and Holland formed a coalition against Louis XIV. The Eastern border was threatened and imperial troop formations moved to Swabia and nearby Breisgau. The French King decided to try to nip a coalition offensive in the bud and in 1673, the Marquis of Vaubrun was ordered by Louvois to take over Colmar. Vaubrun sent the Marquis of Coulanges with 500 cavalrymen to take the city. At the same time, the King was making his way to Brisach and the inhabitants of Colmar, eager not to incur His Majesty's displeasure, removed all their cannons. On Monday 28 August, Louvois arrived at Colmar, to be met by the civic authorities. It was at this moment that Coulanges and his cavalrymen charged into the city through the Deinheim gate. Shortly afterwards, Louvois rode in through the Rouffach gate. Colmar had fallen into the trap and lost everything. The next day, the city was disarmed and the fortifications, the pride of the city, were demolished by a huge gang of some 4,000 men. As a contemporary succinctly put it, "the old city is now as open as a village".

The city was now under French occupation. Troops passed through on their way to the fighting in the Franche-Comté, the Rhine, in Germany. In Autumn 1674, it was the Empire's turn to invade Alsace. The Grand Elector of Brandenburg moved into Colmar, with his wife and some 1,200 men and the city glimpsed a thin flicker of hope, rapidly extinguished by Turenne's victory over the Empire in Turckheim on 5 January 1675. There were now real reasons to be worried

about how Turenne would react to the city's headlong dash into the Elector's arms. Fortunately for them, Turenne spared the city, which, closely watched by the French, hastily decided to keep a low profile.

Little happened for the next four years, until 5 January 1679, five months after the Franche-Comté became part of France, when the Treaty of Nijmegen brought the whole of Alsace under French sovereignty. Colmar was no longer a member of the Holy Roman Empire. In 1680, the baron de Montclar, the Grand Bailiff of Alsace, ordered the old coats of arms to be removed from the city's gates and public buildings. The lys, or lily, replaced the eagle and Colmar had become a Royal City of France.

• **1680** : Religious equality is introduced for all city government jobs, although Protestants still make up some two-thirds of the local population.

• **1683** : The military High Command of Upper Alsace headquarters in Colmar, followed by the Upper Alsace commissioner for war, the regional artillery commissioner, the comptroller of the Royal military hospital and the provincial commissioner for powder and saltpetre.

• **1695** : Colmar is made chef-lieu de subdélégation, the head city for subdelegation, a new territorial division brought in by the Intendant of Alsace.

• **1698** : The Sovereign Council of Alsace is formed in Colmar, making the city the judicial capital of the province of Alsace.

The external tower of the gate of Deinheim or gate of Brisach, 19th c.

The Sovereign Council in Colmar

It is now 22 May 1698. The first meeting of the Sovereign Council to be held in Colmar is taking place in the Wagkeller, the old seat of the patricians. The day began with mass in the Augustinian chapel of the palace. This is where the judges collect their thoughts and pray, alone, before making their appearance in public. The Councillors meet up a few hours later in the assembly room. They are wearing costume and sit down on benches opposite the Presiding judge's seat. The clerk sits next to the Presiding judge, with the bar on the left and the Prosecutor on the right.

Colmar has changed in both status and stature. It is now the seat of the Sovereign Court of Justice for all Alsace and a lot more besides, for the Council is also a Parliament that fashions the future of the province, by bolstering its unity and helping its integration into the Kingdom of France. A lot of ground had been covered since it was created by Royal edict in September 1657 "for the countries and areas ceded to His Majesty by the Treaty of Munster" in 1648.

The Council's task is to assert the King's rights over his new possessions. The King effectively gave the Council the job of "carrying out justice and maintaining our rights without changing any of the laws, constitutions and customs existing up to now in the said area." The Council was initially seated in Ensisheim, the old administrative capital for the Austrian possessions in the region and moved to Ville Neuve Saint-Louis-Les- Brisach on the Rhine in 1681, before settling in Colmar in 1695.

Maating of the Sovereign Council of Alsace, painting by Holdt, 18th century. Unterlinden Museum.

The Sovereign Court was the court of last instance for appeals from lower courts. It also heard legal appeals from ecclesiastical, Protestant and Jewish courts. Its jurisdiction covered a wide area and it handled all cases related to people, whether noble or ecclesiastic. It was the first judge of the so-called "Royal" cases, those cases involving Royal sovereignty or the Catholic religion.

In its role as a Parliament, it registered and officialised acts from central government, papal bulls, personal titles, the statutes of trade and artistic bodies and laws and legislation drawn up by local government. It also oversaw the lower courts and acted as Royal Bailiff and as judge for forestry and water. The Royal mint was also housed there. The Council dispensed justice, to general approval. It defended local customs, while bringing in French laws and jurisprudence. The Sovereign Council helped introduce Colmar to the French way of doing things and brought it onto the national map. Without the Council, which was disbanded at the Revolution, Colmar would not be the administrative and legal capital it is today.

The Council provided some of the first bricks for the construction of the "Colmar model", the meeting-up of a republican tradition with the principles of an absolute monarchy, which provided the basis for the unity of the province, while contributing on a larger scale to the unity of the country itself.

The Palace of the Sovereign Council, illuminated to celebrate the birth of the Dauphin, 10 November 1781, drawing by Schauberger. Colmar municipal library.

The Jesuit church, built by J.J. Sarger.

• **1714** : Colmar acquires the nearby seigniory of Hohlandsbourg and cedes St. Peter's priory to the Jesuits, who had arrived in Colmar in 1698.

• **1735-1744** : A new hospital is built in the city, on the site of the old Franciscan monastery.

• **1742-1750** : Strasbourg architect Jean-Jacques Sarger builds the Jesuit church.

• **1751** : Decker, Colmar printer, publishes the first volume of Alsatia Illustrata by the historian Jean Daniel Schoepflin.

• **1753-1754** : Voltaire, who is doing research on the history of the Empire, spends thirteen months in Colmar.

Voltaire's troubled stay in Colmar

Voltaire stays in Colmar from October 1753 to November 1754, arriving from the court of Frederick II of Prussia. He starts work on the Annales de l'Empire. He makes extensive use of the libraries of the Sovereign Court councillors and lawyers, and comments favourably on the people and their research facilities: "I found in Colmar lawyers who know more about the history of the Empire than anyone in Vienna. People deserving of respect, communicative and with fine libraries that are put entirely at our disposal. I am in the only part of France where you can get help on this subject that no one knows the slightest thing about in Paris."

Voltaire, however, runs up against the hostility of the Jesuits, who contest his worth as a historian and he takes away mixed memories of his stay in Colmar, as can be seen in these comments on the city :

The house where Voltaire lived from 1753 to 1754.

Voltairian anthology

Colmar, a city that is half German, half-French and wholly Iroquian.

The wine and the people of Colmar are excellent indeed, but they have no good cafés.

Colmar is a devout little city, full of annoyance, where everybody goes to confession, where everybody hates each other and where there are no resources save a few lawyers who are well versed in German public law...

Colmar is a singular little city. I was ceremoniously complimented on my going to Easter mass.

Would you believe that it is not without regret that I am leaving Colmar. My bad reputation occasioned me at first to be snubbed by the Holy Church, but all the honest people of the region soon made up for this scandal.

• **1769-1771** : Construction of the Sovereign Council building, designed by Chassain.

Beauties of Colmar

You must go to the plains at harvest-time. This is where you can see as much haymaking as you can pretty girls.

Colmar is perhaps the winner. Breasts appear nicely rounded and white. Eyes are large, the heads full of hair, the mouths full of teeth, the arms fine and elegant and the lips pink and smiling. It is the place where all travellers stop and all regiments want to garrison. Fathers say it was better in their day and that the blood in Colmar is losing its quality. Girls of Colmar, worry you not... your blood is the same, it is the blood of the disgruntled old men that has changed. Your fathers may denigrate you but for the process of beauty, it is the children who decide.

Frédéric-Jacques Masson, Marquis of Pezay
Les soireées hélvétiennes, alsaciennes et franc-comtoises,
London, 1772..

• **1773** : Colmar has 11,280 inhabitants. Théophile Conrad Pfeffel (1736-1809), a poet and teacher, opens a "Military academy".

Statue of Pfeffel by Charles Geiss, 1927.

The Military Academy of Colmar

The academy was military in name only and was only for protestant children of mostly noble descent, who were destined one day perhaps to bear arms. The number of pupils rarely went over 40 and the school seemed bound to fall into discreet obscurity. Within a short time, however, it became known all over Europe and helped increase the fame of the city.

When Pfeffel decided to found his military academy, he was still suffering from the loss of his son, Christian, who is supposed to have appeared to him one night in a dream and encouraged him to start the academy. In fact, Pfeffel had decided on the school well before his son's death, as can be seen from his *Dramatische Kinderspiele*, published in 1769. Another slightly more prosaic reason was quite simply that Pfeffel found he could not live off poetry alone.

Pfeffel founded the academy on the teachings of Basedow, a German native who was influenced by Rousseau, and of baron Salis Marschlin who ran an educational establishment in Graubünden along the lines recommended by Basedow.

"The school accepts children of all families" the academy's promotional pamphlet went, "without regard for their destination or their country of origin ; the only qualities we require of our pupils are a well-born heart, a mind open to culture and a good constitution". In 1781, Pfeffel said of his school: "Our establishment is not an elite school for soldiers or tradesmen, but a breeding ground for all those who want to escape from vulgarity."

Pupils could enter between the ages of 10 and 14. The curriculum lasted three years and covered a number of subjects: languages, history, mathematics, music, fencing, horse-riding and heraldry. The pupils were to be prepared for life in the big, wide world and particular attention was paid to keeping good manners. Their masters would take them to balls and introduce them to the authorities. The uniform, organisation (in companies) and discipline was all along military lines, for the "military" part of the academy needed to be justified. The focus of the teaching, however, was the heart and moral rectitude was considered more important than work and intelligence. The aim was not to teach an elite, but to form honest men: *"instead of wanting to breed intelligent citizens in my kingdom, I should before anything else, have made them into honest citizens"* complained the monarch in the Die Aufklärung fable.

The Military Academy was a considerable success and attracted 288 students in 20 years, a majority of them Swiss, but also Germans, French, Russians, Scots, Swedes and even a single American. The whole of Europe came flocking to Colmar to have a look at this fake military, unashamedly Rousseauist school run by a blind poet. Over a period of 20 years 2,198 people came to Colmar to see the school and sign the poet's Fremdenbuch, including 41 princes, 36 university professors, 28 lawyers and legal experts and 343 women. The list is impressive and made Colmar better known than ever.

• **1775 :** The "La Concorde" Masonic lodge is founded in Colmar. It was made up mainly of members of the Sovereign Council and Army officers and its aims were principally Catholic philanthropy.

Colmar begins to be industrialized. The Haussmann printed cloth factory is founded in Logelbach, a suburb of the city.

"On 17 August 1784, at eight o'clock in the morning in Colmar, at the Deux Clefs, I saw her and was struck dumb with joy."

Vittorio Alfiéri meeting up again with Louise de Stollberg, countess of Albany

- **1785 :** Opening of the "Tabagie littéraire" reading club.

Nothing could be more pleasant than eating at the table d'hôte. The main pleasure is in the diversity of the people sharing your table. In the auberge des Trois Rois, we came across amiable, well-educated and honest people. The dining room was very clean, decorated in the German style; triangular mirrors, framed German quotations, earthenware stoves. We were very well served for 30 s per head. The wine waiter was a young man from Colmar, who did his job skilfully and intelligently, the like of which is rarely seen. We ate several excellent German stews. Most innkeepers are lazy good-for-nothings. The one in Colmar ate with his guests.

Alsace in 1782, an anonymous account.

Pfister House by Michel Hertrich, 1875. Unterlinden Museum.

- **1785-1787** : Pierre Michel d'Ixnard, an architect from Nimes, builds the Salle des actes (theatre) and the library (now part of the Lycée Bartholdi).

- **1787** : The provincial assembly of Alsace is set up in June and Colmar becomes the chief city of one of the six districts initially defined in preparation for the meeting of the States General.

- **1790** : Colmar's population has risen to over 13,000 and it is made departmental capital of the Upper-Rhine department.

Etienne-Ignace Salomon is elected the first mayor of Colmar.

- **1791** : Colmar patriots come together in the Société des Amis de la Constitution and then the Société des Amis de la Liberté et de l'Egalité, affiliated to the Jacobin club of Strasbourg, to discuss the interests of the city and those of the revolutionary movement in general.

Colmar becomes the seat of the constitutional bishopric of the Upper Rhine. St. Martin's collegiate church is made into a cathedral and would remain so until the 1802 concordat.

Place des Dominicains by Michel Hertrich, 1875. Unterlinden Museum.

Colmar would make a charming place for a philosopher to stay. The joviality of the inhabitants and the natural charms of the city and its environs are the very things a wise man seeks.

J. La Vallée, Voyage dans les départements de la France (1792)

- **1792** : Colmar's convents and monasteries are closed down one after the other. The Unterlinden nuns leave the city, after 5 centuries.

- **1793** : Hérault de Séchelles, the representative of the Revolution, turns the Upper Rhine criminal court into a revolutionary court.

13 death sentences are handed out over the next few months.

- **1793-1794** : Bad weather and a succession of poor harvests cause a food shortage, exacerbated by requisitions and the discredited assignat currency.

- **1796** : Opening of the Ecole centrale du Haut-Rhin, the department's first technical college.

- **1800** : The Upper Rhine department's first prefect arrives in Colmar and the city becomes the préfecture capital.

The préfecture by Michel Hertrich, 1876. Unterlinden Museum.

The Upper Rhine préfecture

Since 1791, the departmental capital had been the seat of the constitutional bishopric of the Upper Rhine. Colmar had its own bishop and St. Martin's church was able to claim cathedral status. Less than ten years later, the prefect set up office in Colmar for the first time, thereby bolstering Colmar's position as administrative capital. The Upper Rhine department began to grow. It already included the city of Belfort and its territory, and it was soon also to acquire the department of Mont Terrible, followed in 1800 by the former principality of Porrentruy, Erguel, the provostship of Moutier Granval et Bellay and part of the former principality of Montbéliard, which would remain in Alsace until 1815.

The first Prefect of the Upper Rhine was Jean-Baptiste Harmand, who came from the Meuse and failed to make much of an impression in Colmar. It should be said that he did not really have time on his side as he only lasted eight months in the job before being recalled to Paris after being caught "in a scandalous conflict with his secrétaire général". The next mention of Harmand showed him to be French consul in Santander, Spain. Dismissed during the période des cent jours (the hundred days when Napoleon retook power in 1815), he finished up living in poverty under the Restoration. It was apparently not for nothing that he was known as a "political chameleon", although this description could equally well have applied to just about any of his contemporaries. Political twisting and turning had been turned into an art form between the Revolution and the Restoration.

The préfecture itself was set up in the old abbey of Pairis, the then Town Hall, in 1800. In the same year, Colmar once again became the judicial capital of Alsace and was made the seat of the appeal tribunal (tribunal d'appel), which became an Appeal Court (Cour d'appel) in 1804 and then an Imperial Court in 1810. In April 1800, every French commune found itself headed by a Mayor, after the title had been restored following Napoleon's coup d'état. The new Mayor of Colmar was François Antoine Richter. He worked under the Prefect, Félix Desportes, who would remain in the job from 1802 to 1813 before being thrown out for misappropriating public funds. Between the two of them they helped the city expand beyond its walls. The old city gates were knocked down, which earned the prefect the nickname "gate destroyer". The Champ du Mars military exercise field was changed into a public park. The unfortunate Harmand was credited with producing the original plans for the alleys and shrubs and trees, which were designed in the shape of the légion d'honneur.

- **1803 :** Opening of the Upper Rhine Midwifery school.

- **1804 :** The city once again becomes the regional judicial capital, with a new Appeal Court, which would become an Imperial Court in 1811.

The Lauch by Michel Hertrich, 1874, Unterlinden Museum.

- **1818** : The Herzog textile factory, built next to the Haussmann plant, is constructed, also on the Logelbach canal, to the west of the city.

- **1824** : The Israelite Consistory of Wintzenheim is transferred to Colmar.

The vine is the Queen of this region. It excludes all grass and flowers and deigns only to allow into its court such as potatoes, cabbages, lettuces and other humble vegetables that grow modestly at its feet. The presence of fruit trees is grudgingly suffered, but the vine will haughtily push its grapes up to the height of the fruit on their branches and vie with them for the air.

Colmar was once renowned for the beauty of its fair sex... The upheavals and migrations occasioned by the Revolution have caused the races to mix. Would I say that Colmar has lost nothing with this mix of peoples? Would I say that the beauty of the women has remained unchanged, like Arethusa's spring? Would this gallantry be an avowal of the truth? What do you think, Mesdames? All in all, I prefer you to be judged by your own selves rather than by me.

Pèlerinages d'un Child-harold parisien..., 1825

- **1828** : Royal pomp and splendour as Charles X comes to Colmar.

Another textile factory, Kiener, starts production, in Grillenbreit in the eastern part of the city.

- **1831** : Louis-Philippe, with his two sons, the Dukes of Orleans and Nemours are enthusiastically welcomed in Colmar for their two-day visit on 21 and 22 June 1831.

- **1833** : The departmental Ecole Normale (teacher training college) is set up.

- **1841** : Inauguration of the Basel, Colmar, Strasbourg railway. Colmar's first station is completed the following year, in 1842.

- **1843** : The Jewish community builds a synagogue, rue des Laboureurs.

- **1845** : The city now numbers some 20,000 inhabitants.

- **1847** : The founding of the Société Schongauer which manages the works of art kept in the former convent of Unterlinden.

- **1848** : The Republican society of Colmar shows its colours in the revolution that broke out in February.

Grand-rue, the Arcades by Michel Hertrich, 1876. Unterlinden Museum.

- **1849** : Colmar builds an imposing Italian-style civic theatre next to the Unterlinden museum.

The city of Colmar, while neither beautiful, nor regular in appearance, is pleasant enough, with its magnificent surrounds and the resources that it offers, not unlike those of a larger city, and also its affable, urbane inhabitants. It is not Strasbourg, with its rough Germanic veneer, it is already a French city. The softening of its mores may be attributed to the Royal court, as may its fuller, wider education and the good sense of its societies. The city still boasts some of the old monuments that were its glory in times gone past.

Joseph-Sybille de Chevery, Histoire d'Alsace, 1849

- **1854** : Cholera strikes Colmar, making 349 victims.

The Lauch, Petite Venise by Michel Hertrich, 1874. Unterlinden Museum.

Cholera in Colmar

The last epidemic of a long list and also the best documented as we can now see the figures in official documents as opposed to relying on folklore and legend. The records show that 505 people out of the total population of 21,348 were infected, 349 of whom died. Although in absolute terms the numbers do not seem so terrifying, the actual effect the epidemic had on the population was devastating. The disease had a profoundly traumatising effect on both those living in the depths of poverty and the people who thought they had the ways and means to halt its march. Was cholera a disease that struck only the poor who lived in conditions of abject hygiene ?

On the face of it, the answer was yes. Cholera was known to have come across from Asia, hitting the world in six successive waves from 1817 onwards. Cholera was always transmitted orally and was carried in the water, the quality of which was therefore a determining factor in the spread of the disease. In Colmar, like everywhere else, water was used for drinking, cleaning and for washing food.

Rue de l'église by Michel Hertrich, 1876. Unterlinden Museum.

The reports from the 1830's, when cholera was rife in Europe, painted an appalling picture. Documents of the Sanitary Intendance of the Upper Rhine showed that both rural and urban streets and houses were in a filthy state. Stables, dungheaps and latrines inside the houses created ideal conditions for the proliferation of the virus. Although public buildings were cleaned with chlorinated water and painted with lime, few private houses went to the same pains. Hygiene precautions recommended by the Mayor went largely ignored.

The hardest hit of all were the people living in narrow, airless streets like the rue de la Herse, rue de la Poissonnerie, rue de la Harth and rue Haslinger. 174 of the 349 people who died in the outbreak were factory workers and another 104 were day labourers. When a commission of enquiry was set up in the aftermath of the epidemic, its findings showed that few of the houses in the city had a cesspool, while faeces were often simply dumped in courtyards or thrown directly into the water running through the city. Essential water purification was continually being put off, with the city council not wanting to make itself unpopular with the local population by levying further taxes to cover the costs.

1856 : Bartholdi carves the statue of General Rapp. Opening of the Lycée impérial de Colmar.

1863 : Jean Macé, a teacher in Beblenheim, a village near Colmar, founds the communal library society of the Upper Rhine (Société des bibliothèques communales du Haut-Rhin).

1869 : The Colmar-Munster railway line is built.

It is a city of tradition, study and conscience. The Colmar bourgeoisie makes strenuous efforts to conserve the houses of their fathers, their libraries, their cellars and their faith. The men are God-fearing, enlightened and thoughtful: they are not dismissive of comfort, they are thrifty, they care not for idle luxury or for noise. Their days count at least 24 hours, each person filling them as best they think fit; nobody seems to find them overlong...

Edmond About, Alsace 1871-1872

1870 : Colmar's population climbs to nearly 24 000 and the city founds its first Chamber of Commerce. In September, groups of irregulars and volunteers, including Bartholdi the sculptor, fight against the Baden troops.

1871 : The Treaty of Frankfurt of 10 May 1871 sees Alsace come under German rule. Colmar remains the departmental capital, but is subordinate to the provincial Government in Strasbourg.

Colmar in the Reichsland

The Treaty of Frankfurt, signed on 10 May 1871, saw France cede Alsace and the Moselle to Germany, thereby bringing to an end the Franco-German war which had been waged since 19 July 1870. The Empire of Napoleon III collapsed, to be replaced by the new German Empire.

Alsace was the scene of a whole series of bloody combats, notably at Morsbronn, Froeschwiller and Reichshoffen. These villages are known in French history as the pockets of a heroic resistance, which was, however, not enough to stave off defeat. One of the sorriest episodes of the war was the bombardment of Strasbourg and the destruction of the library, containing Herrad of Landsberg's famous Hortus deliciarum, one of the finest manuscripts of the 12th century. Colmar put up brave, but vain resistance, while Bartholdi and his fellow volunteers fought valiantly at the bridge of Horbourg on 14 September 1870.

Colmar found itself up against overwhelming numerical superiority and was captured by the Baden troops. The French military authorities, refusing an open battle, ordered the garrison to fall back to the Vosges. Mayor Peyerimhoff was made responsible for keeping order in the city and he declared Colmar to be an open city. There then followed a period of uncertainty, with the city hovering anxiously between French and German domination before the first German officials marched in. The city council was kept in office, while the elections to the French constitutional assembly, which the occupying forces allowed to go ahead, were won by the patriotic list. This was no last gesture of defiance before the Treaty of Frankfurt. The highly liberal provisions of the Treaty allowed the inhabitants to opt for keeping French nationality; 3,587 of whom promptly did so (15 % of the population). Bartholdi himself took an oath never to return to his native city (an oath he was later to break).

Colmar therefore became part of Germany. The German administration sensibly enough allowed the city to remain the administrative capital of the region. The new Bezirk had the same boundaries as the old département, minus the Territory of Belfort, while the Court of Appeal also remained in the city (although it avoided being transferred by the skin of its teeth). By 1875, the population had reached its previous level, with 23,999 inhabitants. The exodus had been compensated for by immigration, mostly of Government officials and by regular demographic growth.

- **1877** : Mayor Hercule Peyerimhoff is replaced by a German commissar. The move does not go down at all well in Colmar.

- **1882** : The Société d'embellissement is created to "embellish the city". Among its many acts, it commissions a number of statues from Bartholdi, most of which are still to be seen today around the squares and streets of the city.

- **1883** : French is banned in official documents. Alsatian civil servants are thought unreliable and are restricted to low-ranking positions.

- **1884-1886** : Colmar's water supply is completely renewed and an imposing new water tower built in the southern part of the city.

The winemaker by Bartholdi, 1869.

A fairly handsome French city, gay and with pleasant walks: such is the first impression we are given by Colmar. In the evening, families stroll along the promenades. The old part of town, with its curious houses, is lively enough. Before going home, whole families will stop by in a brasserie. And once night falls, the city streets empty, leaving only a handful of soldiers flirting with servant girls.

By ten o'clock only the sentries remain, their footsteps echoing off the doors of the military commanders or the German authorities.

Maurice Fauste, Là-bas, promenade en Alsace en 1885...

• **1888 :** Construction of the barracks along the route de Strasbourg.

• **1898 :** The Colmar wine Institute is founded. One of its main aims is to prevent the spread of phylloxera and other diseases that ravage local vines.

• **1900 :** Inauguration of St. Joseph's church, in a new district to the west of the railway line.

Colmar's population has now reached 36,844.

• **1902 :** A tram line is built between the station and the canal. In 1904, the tram carried 668 000 passengers, which led the authorities to build a second line between the route de Basel and the route de Strasbourg, inaugurated in 1914. The development of public transport went some way towards meeting the burgeoning demands of urban expansion.

The tramway at the beginning of the rue des Clefs, early 20th c.

- **1906** : Colmar builds brand new Municipal Baths, right by the Unterlinden museum.

- **1907** : The new station, with a profile described by Colmar artist Hansi as "highly reminiscent of an elegant locomotive", is opened to traffic.

- **1908** : Official visit of Kaiser Wilhelm II.

- **1910** : Colmar now has 43,800 inhabitants including 4,000 soldiers.

Narrow, fickle roads, filled at night, houses with great sloping roofs with red tiles weathered by time, houses with mansard roofs wherein the architect has managed to conjure an extra floor, houses with gabled roofs, crenelated or festooned, aligned at the builder's whim, with the upper floor overhanging the ground floor, small windows with green shutters, some of the houses sticking out potbellied, some stooped with all askew, drawn tightly up like old women, with a truly human look; others are more delicate, the houses of civic worthies, often with white plaster and exposed beams, a sculpted gate, a turret: and in the silence of the night, the effect can be startling. The houses are of an extraordinary variety, with facades born of the imagination...

Paul Acker, Colmar, 1910

Colmar train station.

As soon as one enters within the city of Colmar, one knows one is in a city of history,
that takes great care to keep intact the precious reserves left to it over the centuries:
reserves of glory, reserves of art, reserves of liberty. Colmar was once a free city and
has not forgotten it. Colmar was once a French city and still remembers it.

André Hallays, 1912

- **1914** : On 23 August, French cavalry patrols ride into Colmar. Hopes of liberation prove short-lived as the French Army pulls back into the Vosges mountains.

- **1917** : On 8 August, four people are killed by French bombardments and the municipal baths and the Unterlinden school severely damaged. The war is drawing near to the city. On 16 September there is a spectacular dogfight above the city pitting French fighters against 14 German planes from the Colmar base.

- **1918** : On Armistice Day, 11 November, a soviet is proclaimed, made up of a mix of soldiers' and workmen's committees. French troops enter the city on 18 November.

Military review, place Rapp, 18 November 1918, by Victor Huen.

The triumphal tricolore

"In all the years of my long life, I have never witnessed such popular enthusiasm as that which we experienced during the days after the liberation of 18 November. Regiments marched into Colmar, one after the other, in the midst of an indescribable frenzy of waving flags and heaving crowds. And all around one could see Alsatian women dressed up in traditional costumes in the blue, white and red of the French tricolore, that they had hastily sewn together to be able to greet their liberators. Government leaders and army marshals such as Clemenceau, Poincaré, Joffre and Foch, were all welcomed over the next few weeks with a fervour and warmth as had never before been seen."

Joseph Rey, the Mayor of Colmar from 1947 to 1977, had, like thousands of other Colmarians, witnessed the heady first days of the liberation. After the hardships and mourning of the five previous years, they could at last let themselves go and the whole city launched itself into a huge celebration, ignoring the last few German nationals who had yet to leave the city. Colmar had generously opened its arms. France suddenly became the symbol of all virtues under the sun and heaven, a land bedecked by the three-coloured flag. The walls were covered in posters and proclamations printed in blue, white and red. Extravagant garlands hung between the houses and a joyous crowd had taken over the city, singing and chanting in the few words of French they knew. "Crowds of young people were singing with the Alsatian accent "Fife la France, merte la Prusse, Fife la République".

"And regiments of infantry marched past and then marched back again, headed by a band playing "Vous n'aurez pas l'Alsace et la Lorraine", followed by squadrons of cavalry, riding with drawn sabres and accompanied by trumpets sounding out lively fanfares" (Pierre Burger). The crowd was in the streets or gathered at the windows, cheering the infantry and cavalry as they made their way through the city, the wheels of the artillery trailers and the great cannons thundering along behind them. Girls dressed up in Alsatian costume and local associations with banners proudly unfurled marched gaily behind the military might. On 22 November the celebrations started afresh, for the visit of Raymond Poincaré, the President of France and Georges Clémenceau, the Prime Minister. There seemed no end to the revelry.

- **1919** : The 152nd regiment of Foot and the 11th regiment of Dragoons are posted to Colmar.

- **1922** : A public agency for low-cost housing is set up to try and cope with the acute housing shortage.

- **1924** : Colmar becomes the seat of the Agricultural Chamber of the Upper Rhine.

- **1928** : The "Colmar Trial" of the leaders of the Alsatian autonomist movement, follo-wing the Alsatian malaise aroused, among other things, by the declarations of Edouard Herriot, the then Prime Minister, on 17 June 1924, when he attempted to speed up the application of the whole of the French legal code in Alsace. This

caused considerable protest in Alsace, where concern was mounting over the threat to the region's confessional status.

- **1936** : Colmar's population reaches 49,448 inhabitants.

- **1937** : Inauguration of the new Louis Pasteur hospital.

- **1939** : 1st September, France is at war again.

- **1940** : On 17 June, the Germans roll into Colmar and Alsace is annexed. On 30 August, the Rapp monument is destroyed, followed on 9 September by the Bruat monument. A brutal Germanization and Nazification programme comes into force.

A resistance network is formed in November, helping escaped prisoners of war pass over the Vosges.

- **1942** : Everybody between the ages of 10 and 18 is forced to join the Hitler youth (2 January).

The Germans break up the Colmar resistance network and throw the leaders into prison.

On 25 August, military service becomes obligatory in Alsace and Moselle. In blatant disregard of international laws and human decency, 130,000 young men are forced to wear the uniforms of the Wehrmacht and the Waffen SS. 40,000 of them would die in the battles.

• **1944** : An ammunition train blows up in the goods station on 18 September, causing considerable damage over a 1-kilometer radius. The same night, police swoops bring in around fifty local figures who are subsequently deported to Germany.

• **1945** : On 2 February, the city is liberated after fierce fighting around the "Colmar pocket". General de Gaulle marches into the city on 10 February, and General Rapp's statue is later restored to its rightful pedestal.

General de Gaulle first came to Colmar on 10 February 1945, returning on 20 November 1959 as President of the Republic.

The Liberation of Colmar

The 2 February 1945 is a key date in the city's history. For the citizens of Colmar, it marked the end of the war, even if fighting continued for a time elsewhere in Europe. The battle of the Colmar pocket was the last to be fought on French soil. Three whole months would pass between the liberation of Strasbourg and that of Colmar, with desperate German resistance holding up the Allied advance before finally collapsing. The operation was supposed to have been all over within a short time. In November 1944, General De Lattre de Tassigny's 1st Army launched a crushing offensive in the south of Alsace that broke through the German front line to take Belfort and then pushed on to the Rhine, liberating Mulhouse on 21 November.

Two days later, General Leclerc's 2nd armoured division entered Strasbourg, after a campaign that had started in Koufra in Chad. The liberation of Alsace now seemed just a question of days or even hours. The panic-stricken Nazi authorities in Colmar had already fled the city and the Colmarians were getting ready to celebrate their liberation. But then the Americans wavered and De Lattre decided to call a halt to his offensive in the plain of Alsace and withdraw the 5th armoured division to the rear of the French lines. The German reaction was swift. Operation Nordwind was launched on 1 January

1945 in the north of Alsace, as part of the German counter-attack that had already successfully regained the initiative in the Ardennes since 16 December 1944.

In Upper Alsace, since December, the French troops had been halted to the north of Mulhouse and to the south of Ribeauvillé and Riquewihr. On 22 January 1945, despite the freezing cold and the snow, General de Lattre launched a pincer-movement to liberate Colmar and reach the Rhine at Brisach. Colmar was surrounded from the north and the west. General Schlesser's daring night attack on 1 and 2 February brought the French army into Colmar and the city was at long last liberated.

Fighting in the Colmar pocket would continue until 9 February. The battle itself had lasted twenty one days in freezing conditions and resulted in heavy Allied losses, with 8,000 American dead and 16,000 French. The German 19th Army, under General Raspe, lost over 20,000 men, with a further 16,000 being taken prisoner.

- **1946 :** Colmar is decorated with the croix de guerre 1939-1946 with bar.

- **1947 :** As part of the decentralization of French theatre, initiated by Jeanne Laurent, the Deputy Director at the Ministry for the Arts, the Centre dramatique de l'Est is formed in Colmar.

  Joseph Rey becomes Mayor of Colmar and will remain in office for thirty years, making a vital contribution to the city's development.

- **1948 :** The first Regional Wine Fair is held in Colmar. The event will soon become a flagship both for the local economy and for regional tourism.

- **1958 :** The Colmar industrial zone is created to the north of the city.

Colmar's industrial zone, as it is now.

A new industrial zone

The industrial zone to the north of the city was set up to boost the city's industrial development.

The turning point in the city's industrialization came with the decision by American roller bearing manufacturer Timken to set up their new European production facilities in Colmar. The opening of the Timken plant in May 1959 showed that Colmar was ready to play its role in a genuinely modern industrial society. Fifty four European cities and towns had been in competition for Timken and the company's directors had travelled some 300,000 kilometres in search of the ideal location. It took the untiring work of the Mayor of Colmar and all his staff, along with a highly-detailed, attractive development plan to persuade the Americans to opt for the warmth and welcome of the city.

Things now started to move forward apace and over 30 more companies were to set up in Colmar over the next 10 years, thereby creating some 4,000 new jobs and taking the city out of the single-industry syndrome that had so nearly proved fatal before.

The industrial zone was extended eastwards and then to the south, with some 500 hectares available for industrial development. A wide variety of companies were now working within the area, from a number of different sectors, including textile, mechanical engineering, public works, agribusiness, earthenware and ceramics, pharmaceuticals and electronics.

In 1960, fresh opportunities were to be had with the opening of the Colmar-Neuf-Brisach port on the Rhine. The new facilities, operated by the chamber of commerce meant that Middle Alsace was now ideally placed to take advantage of its geographical location and to develop closer ties with both the rest of the European Community and farther afield.

The growth in industry also had a highly salutary effect on the city's finances, with business taxes now accounting for some 60 % of local tax revenue.

By 1980, the city's northern industrial zone had managed to attract 66 companies, employing over 7,000 people.

The west of the city, as it is now.

• **1959** : The city creates a new housing belt to the east that would be completed ten years later and house 12,000 people.

• **1960** : Opening of the Colmar-Neuf-Brisach Rhine port.

• **1963** : Pierre Pflimlin, the President of the Council of Europe's Consular Assembly, presented Colmar with the European Flag of Honour in a ceremony held in front of Matthias Grunewald's of Issenheim altarpiece in the Unterlinden museum.

• **1964** : Opening of Colmar-Houssen airport.

Creation of the Communauté d'intérêt Moyenne Alsace-Brisgau, a pilot body set up to foster cross-border economic cooperation and development.

• **1966** : : A decision taken at Ministerial level makes a large part of the old town of Colmar a listed historical monument, protected by the law.

• **1968** : The restoration of the quartier des tanneurs (the tanners' district), begins and will be finished in 1974. Inauguration of the exhibition centre in the north of the city. The university faculty takes in its first students.

The Atelier lyrique du Rhin, part of the Opéra du Rhin, a regional opera company covering Strasbourg, Mulhouse and Colmar, is brought to Colmar.

Spectacular restoration works

The restoration of the tanners' district is the best known and most spectacular of the work carried out in Colmar. The operation began in 1968, was completed in 1974 and involved thirty-three properties, all rundown and in urgent need of renovation. Twenty-seven of the properties were restored, creating some one hundred and eight luxury apartments and sixteen office units.

A lot of Colmarians still remember the spectacular restoration work. The buildings were laid bare, stripped down to their wooden framework, and the brickwork thoroughly cleaned, before the start of the actual restoration work. The interior design and layout no longer had anything to do with original structures, while the installation of lifts inside the buildings also caused a few heads to turn.

While the technical part of the restoration work went off without any particular snags, the social aspect caused a profound upheaval in the district. The 150 or so people living in the district were aging and of modest means and the housing was not up to the required standard. They were moved out and housed elsewhere in the city.

The whole area, previously little more than a rundown cluster of old houses, was turned into a residential district for three hundred and fifty people, mostly managers in local companies who had moved to Colmar for their jobs. Both the inhabitants and the social status of the tanners' district had completely changed.

The "quartier des tanneurs", a village within the city, has now become a magnet for tourists and has brought millions of visitors to the city from all over the world.

- **1972 :** The City Council extends the listed area to cover practically the whole of the old city. Work begins on St. Martin's collegiate church, to be finished in 1985.

- **1974 :** 22 June - the legendary Pink Floyd concert in the exhibition park packs in 12,000 fans.

Woodstock at Colmar !

It was just a few years ago, but it already seems like ages. 5 short years in the city's history, 1974-1978, but five years that had an enormous impact on the music scene both in Colmar and over the whole of the region. Organised by Colmarian Thierry Rohmer, the festival formed a gigantic "who's who" of 70's rock legends that'll stay for ever in the memories of those lucky enough to be at the concerts.

Pink Floyd, Jethro Tull, Wallenstein, Slade, Genesis, Lou Reed, Rory Gallagher, Van der Graff Generator, Ange, Manfred Mann, The Who, Uriah Heep, Kraftwerk, Ritchie Blackmore's Rainbow, Magma, Tangerine Dream, Santana, Status quo, Black Sabbath, U.F.O, Peter Gabriel, Frank Zappa, Blue OysterCult and a whole host of others. The rock fan's dream.

There were 12,000 people at Pink Floyd's 22 June concert in 1974, with hair flowing down their backs, faded jeans and bare feet, gathered in Colmar's open-air theatre to listen, dance and celebrate the music. Roads all around were jammed solid and it seemed like the whole world had come to the city's own Woodstock.

- **1975 :** Colmar's population climbs to 67,410 inhabitants and the first pedestrian precinct is opened.

- **1978 :** The number of visitors in one year to the Unterlinden museum tops the 350,000 mark, making it the most popular regional museum in France.

- **1979 :** Colmar inaugurates its International Music Festival in the Dominican church, under the baton of German conductor Karl Münchinger.

- **1983 :** The city is twinned with Eisenstadt, capital of Burgenland in Austria, a winemaking town that was home to Joseph Haydn.

- **1987 :** Colmar twins with Princeton, the famous American university town, the day after the hundredth anniversary of the Statue of Liberty, sculpted by Colmar's Auguste Bartholdi.

- **1989 :** Russian conductor and violinist Vladimir Spivakov takes over as Director of the International Music Festival, which soon gains a well-deserved international reputation.

Vladimir Spivakov, director of the Colmar International Music Festival.

• **1990** : The Théâtre de la Manufacture opens in the old tobacco production building, which houses L'atelier du Rhin, the regional drama centre and lyrical workshop, part of the Opéra du Rhin.

• **1993** : The Colmar I.U.T. (Technical University) with its four teaching faculties, wins its independence within the Université de Haute-Alsace.

Colmar is twinned with Györ, a historical Hungarian city with a population of 120,000, situated between Vienna and Budapest.

• **1995** : The Colmar by-pass opens, bringing to an end the last bottleneck on the main north-south road-link in Alsace.

• **1996** : The André Malraux contemporary Art Gallery opens. Two major new cultural events are inaugurated: the jazz festival and the "7 days for the 7th art" film festival.

• **1997** : The Old Town is given a facelift and the old streets renovated. The work on St. Matthew's church, a former Franciscan church, is completed. Colmar launches a spectacular and ambitious programme using attractive light arrangements to enhance the city's heritage.

Restored, St. Mathew's church hosts the International Music Festival.

- **1999** : A vast residential renovation programme is initiated by Gilbert Meyer, mayor of Colmar since 1995, to improve the western part of the city. The first stage involves the Palais Royal district.

- **2000** : Colmar's theatre is completely refurbished, a redesigned, car-free Place Rapp and an extended, modernised open-air theatre in the exhibition park.

Inside the theatre

The theatre gets a facelift !

- **2002 :** The city of Colmar becomes a member of the UNICEF network, a child-friendly city.

- **2004 :** Commemoration of the centenary of the death of the sculptor Auguste Bartholdi (Colmar 1834 - Paris 1904). The city of Colmar erects a copy of the Statue of Liberty 12 metres in height (made by Guillaume Roche) to pay him homage (located on the Route de Strasbourg).

The forecourt of the railway station is redeveloped in order to enhance the frontage of the building.

Construction around the old brick chimney at the library and buildings of the IUT Grillenbreit, the remains of the industrial site. Preservation of the urban memory of past industrial activity in the development of the university campus.

- **2007 :** Since 10 June, the city of Colmar has been connected to the TGV Est high speed railway network. The service enables several return journeys to Paris each day.

- **2008:** In the context of the Urban Renovation Scheme, the opening up of the railway station to the west is an important step. An ambitious social and urban requalification project in the Europe neighbourhood.

- **2009 :** The Book Fair celebrates its 20th anniversary ! This literary event is the most important in Alsace.

Colmar is the finish town for the 13th stage of the Tour de France and the start town the following day. Each time the Tour passes through the city, it arouses immense interest in spectators.

1 July : The water sports centre on the site of the north Holcim gravel pit is opened to the public (during the works, remains dating back to the Neolithic period are uncovered).

The open air theatre at the Exhibition Complex, nicknamed «the shell», with seating for an audience of 10,000 people, becomes a must for the summer music tours.

• **2010 :** The President of the Republic, Nicolas Sarkozy, celebrates the 65th anniversary of the victory of 8 May 1945 in Colmar.

Colmar is awarded the Marianne d'Or for sustainable development.

Rehabilitation of the permanent covered market. Twenty or so traders share this vibrant new environment in Colmar, giving pride of place to locally produced quality products.

Inauguration of the Liebherr factory on the site of the former aerodrome.

• **2011 :** The eastern branch of the TGV Rhine-Rhone line is put into service between Dijon and Mulhouse, linking Colmar to Lyons.

Renovation of the Exhibition Complex and creation of a modular conference area capable of seating 300 to 1400 people.

• **2012 :** Inauguration of the Edmond Gerrer media and culture Centre (PMC), which is one of the biggest in France. After the National Library of France, the PMC houses the most impressive collection of incunabula

Laying of the first stone for the extension works on the Unterlinden Museum by Gilbert Meyer, Mayor of Colmar, which represents a major project for the city's urban planning and its qualities as a tourist attraction. The project has been entrusted to the famous architects from Basel, Herzog & de Meuron.

65th edition of the Wine Fair. Johnny Halliday gives the opening concert on this occasion.

Liebherr undertakes the extension of the Alsatian site barely a year and a half after its inauguration, creating new jobs to boot.

2013 : The Colmar International Festival celebrates its 25th birthday under the artistic direction of the maestro, Vladimir Spivakov.

Figures in Colmar's history

Roesselmann, the hero

Jean Roesselmann, provost of Colmar, was thrown out of the city in 1260 by nobles acting for Walter de Geroldseck, the bishop of Strasbourg, who wanted Colmar to become part of his dominion. He managed to smuggle his way back in, hidden in a barrel, to free the city from the nobles' grasp. When the bishop again tried to take Colmar, Roesselmann put up a heroic resistance, fighting off the bishop's forces and losing his own life in the process. Ever since, he has held a special position in Colmar's history, as the defender of the city's liberties and her first hero.

Martin Schongauer, the artist of Colmar

Martin Schongauer (ca.1450 -1491) is the best-known of the Colmar artists. His Virgin of the Rose Bush (1473), housed in the Dominican church, is considered his masterpiece. He made his name, however, as an engraver and was known throughout mediaeval Europe, influencing major artists such as Dürer. Schongauer was at his peak at the same time as the printing press was invented and it was the sudden and widespread availability of printed material that spread his fame.

Georges Wickram, the father of the popular novel

Georges Wickram (ca.1500-1562) is considered the father of the popular novel in German literature. The characters in Rollwagenbüchlein (1555), his most famous work, came straight out of a typical slice of mediaeval life, with craftsmen, barbers, tailors, innkeepers, peasants and lansquenets. Wickram had a large output and also wrote dramas and carnival plays that would often be performed in Colmar. He also managed to find the time to run a well-known singing school.

Pfeffel... the European

Théophile Conrad Pfeffel (1736-1809) is best known for his fables and he is sometimes called the Alsatian La Fontaine. He used the fables to put across his political and social message. In 1773, Pfeffel opened his "Military Academy" in Colmar, based on the most advanced pedagogical principles of the time. People came to the city from all over Europe to see the academy.

Jean Daniel Schumacher, the Tsar's librarian

Schumacher was born in Colmar in 1690. He was invited to St. Petersburg by Peter the Great to become the Tsar's official librarian. From 1725 until his death in 1758, he was also the irremovable general secretary of the city's Academy of Science, which the Tsar had decided would be the driving force behind the country's research and education policy. His introduction to the Tsar came about as a result of his marrying the daughter of Peter's head chef !

Jean-François Reubell... our only Head of State !

Reubell (1747-1807) was the only Alsatian to have ever occupied the highest office in the land over a long period. Originally a lawyer in the Sovereign Council, he represented the Haut-Rhin department in the Constituent Assembly (1789-1791), then at the Convention (1792-1795). He was a member of the Committee for Public Safety and the Committee for General Security (1794-1795) before becoming Directeur de la République (1795-1799). His portfolio in the Directory included Finance and Foreign Affairs and he made a significant contribution to the policy of annexing the countries on the left bank of the Rhine and the incorporation of Belgium.

Rapp, Napoleon's intrepid general

Jean Rapp (1771-1821) is the most popular figure in the city's history. Colmar is known locally as the "city of Rapp". A hero of Napoleon's Grand Army, he was wounded 22 times and was famous for his unflinching bravery. Rapp was involved in all Napoleon's major campaigns and was his aide-de-camp before being appointed Governor of Danzig and then Peer of France and Chamberlain to Louis XVIII. He never renounced his loyalty to Napoleon, even when serving under Louis. When Napoleon died in 1821, Rapp was so inconsolable that Louis came to comfort him in person, saying "Do not be embarrassed, Rapp, I hope you will cry as much for me". He was, however, only to outlive Bonaparte by a few months.

Bruat, the sailor

Armand Joseph Bruat (1796-1855), Colmar born and bred, found glory in the battle of Navarino in 1827, when the ship he captained rammed the Turkish admiral's flagship. He was appointed Governor of the Marquesas Islands in 1843, commanded the French squadron in the Pacific Ocean and established the French protectorate in Queen Pomaré's Polynesian territories. Napoleon III promoted him to "Amiral de France" after the fall of Sebastopol in the Crimean War, when he was the commander of the French fleet in the Black Sea. Bruat fell victim to cholera on his way back to France in 1855.

Auguste Bartholdi, the sculptor of the Statue of Liberty

Auguste Bartholdi (1834-1904) is the best-known of all 19th-century Alsatian artists. Although he achieved world-wide celebrity for his Statue of Liberty at the entrance to New York (1886), Bartholdi also designed the Terreaux fountain in Lyons, the Lion of Belfort and the statue of Vercingetorix in Clermont-Ferrand. It should be said that nowadays, the fame of the Statue of Liberty has far outgrown that of its sculptor.

Hansi the misunderstood

Jean-Jacques Waltz (1871-1951), best-known as Hansi, was an artist and cartoonist whose often satirical drawings paint an evocative picture of German-occupied Alsace in the period before and during the First World War. His Alsace was an idyllic, rural, dreamlike region whose folksy images were rapidly taken up to satisfy political, economic and tourist needs.

Legends and stories of Colmar

The club of Hercules

Hercules, the half-God, on his way back from the garden of Hesperides, found himself in the region between the Vosges and the Rhine, that would later become Alsace. It was late, he was hot and he had a great thirst upon him. Entering an inn, he downed vast quantities of the local wine which was reputed even then and thereupon fell into a deep sleep, his head spinning. When he came to the next morning, his head was aching and he saw that his herd had run off during the night. Rushing off in hot pursuit, he left his club behind.

The locals, with their love of all things tidy, eventually placed the forgotten club in the town's coat of arms. This probably explains why, for as long as can be remembered, the inhabitants of Colmar have been known as the Kolbnarren – the mad clubmen.

The phantom of the dairy

If you lie in wait patiently, on certain nights in the rue des Augustins, just next to the prison of Colmar, you can espy the pale, furtive outline of a woman clothed all in white, the phantom of the dairy. The poor woman, many, many years ago, was caught adding water to her milk and God, from a sense of justice, obliged her to return every night, in her penitent's garb, to throw the offending liquid into the well of the Augustinians.

The beast of Colmar

The better-informed visitor to Colmar knows that it is best to steer clear of the rue des Clefs at certain hours of the night. The street, by day a bustling shopping area (the Town Hall is also in the same street) at night becomes the haunt of a terrifying calf, the famous Colmar Nachtkalb. No one knows exactly how long he has been playing his evil tricks, lowing mightily from his hiding place and sometimes charging poor animals that have wandered away from the safety of their homes or tourists staggering out of the local wistubs, their bellies full of the local wine.

The mysterious horse with no body

Seldom seen, but even more terrifying, on certain days of the year around midnight, there can be heard whinnying and the clattering of hooves on some stairways, heralding the fleeting glimpse of the bodiless, emaciated head of a galloping nag.

The four riots of Colmar

The people of Colmar are, generally speaking, a peace-loving bunch and it is rare for them to resort to violence. However, in the space of 22 years, between 1833 and 1855, the population rose up no fewer than four times to defend their rights. The Bubberi riots, the firewood riots, the cucumber riots and the hearse riots had a profound effect on the local psyche, for they were the reaction of simple folk whose modest rights had come under threat.

The Bubberi riots

The local market gardeners and winemakers used to drink a wine that was made purely to quench their considerable thirst. This Bubberi, as it was known, had little to do with normal wine and was not to be found outside the local haunts. One day in 1833, the tax people decided it would be a good idea to slap a hefty 22 sols per hectoliter tax on the stuff, the same as for a normal wine. The idea backfired. At the end of October, discontent grew into open revolt and spread from the Krutenau to the centre of the city, where the winemakers and market-gardeners were joined by workers from local factories. Barricades were thrown up and stones hurled at the local soldiery, called out to control the crowd. The enraged townsfolk threatened to drag the Head of Taxation, the vicomte de Croismare, out into the street, throw him into a barrel of Bubberi and then pour the whole lot into the Sinn (the local river). The national guard was summoned, but they steadfastly refused to charge their fellow-citizens. It was finally only with the intervention of the Prefect and the army that order was restored. The Viscount was dismissed, the tax abolished and the imprisoned ringleaders acquitted. No one would ever again try to tax the Bubberi.

The firewood riot

Nine years later, the city council, running short of cash, decided to tax the wood which local people, especially the poorest, would, for a token payment, gather from the forests to heat their houses. The move went down badly and in June 1842, the people decided to occupy Mayor Chappuis' town hall in protest. The leaders were arrested and thrown into jail. The next day, a sale of wood in the Niederwald forest was interrupted by an excited bunch of locals, somewhat the worse for drink. Encouraged by their initial success, they decided to march into the city with the firm intention of seizing the Mayor, who, panic-stricken, called in a squadron of lancers from Selestat, along with 4 companies of the 7th line regiment of Strasbourg. The money raised by the tax was gobbled up by the expense of having all the troops in the city. The affair cost the city council all its credit.

The cucumber riot

In 1854, at the height of the cholera epidemic, which had a devastating effect on Colmar, the authorities, scared stiff by the deplorable conditions of hygiene in certain districts and the subsequent risks of contagion, decided to turn their attention to the food the inhabitants of Colmar were eating. One of the victims of the new measures was the cucumber. This hardly went down well with the market-gardeners who grew the stuff. Among them were three sisters, "filthy, ugly old maids", who first verbally, and then physically, assaulted the sergeant of the city who had come on an unannounced visit to the market. The sergeant and his escort were bombarded with cucumbers, marrows, turnips and Jerusalem artichokes by the three furies, who were rapidly joined by their fellow market-gardeners. It needed the intervention of the police and the army before order could be restored. For Mayor Chappuis, who had already been through the firewood riots, this was one more he could sorely have done without.

The hearse riot

The hearse riot, in 1855, proved fatal for Mayor Chappuis. Up till then, the good people of Colmar had gone to their final resting place, the Rappendantz (literally "the place where the ravens dance") with the help of local carpenters, locksmiths, sculptors and porters, who would join forces to make the final journey as fine and comfortable as possible and bring in a little extra income at the same time. The "funeral band" as they were known, did not at all appreciate the city's initiative in handing over responsibility for burials to the newly-founded undertakers' association. They had no difficulty in bringing the locals over to their side, making out the city wanted to stop them burying their own dead. Burials conducted by the professional undertakers were attacked and had to have a police escort. The prefect did not like the look of any of this and ended up sacking poor old Mayor Chappuis. It was an excellent excuse for getting rid of a mayor who, as everyone remembered, had unconvincingly switched from being a republican in 1848 to a Napoleonite under Napoleon III. His long period in office finally came to an end as his popularity had run out.

FOR ANY INFORMATION, PLEASE CONTACT
Office de Tourisme
4, rue des Unterlinden
68000 COLMAR
Tél. 00 33 (0)3 89 20 68 92 • Fax. 00 33 (0) 3 89 41 34 13

Auteur : Gabriel BRAEUNER
Photos : Christophe HAMM
Conception graphique : Philippe De Melo & Damien Schitter

Crédit photos :
Octave ZIMMERMANN, photographe du Musée Unterlinden, page 4
Musée d'histoire Naturelle, pages 30 et 31
Musée du Jouet, page 50
Festival Internationnal de Colmar, pages 52, 109
Festival international de Colmar - création graphique Freddy Ruhlmann, page 110
Musée Bartholdi « Christian KEMPF », page 121
Patrick FLESCH, archives municipales de Colmar

I.D. L'Édition
9, rue des Artisans - 67210 Bernardswiller
Tél. 03 88 34 22 00 - Fax : 03 88 34 26 26
info@id-edition.com - www.id-edition.com
Coproduction Office de Tourisme de Colmar

ISBN : 2-913302-58-0
Dépôt légal : nouvelle édition - décembre 2018